D0710185

Dale Carnegie's Radio Program:

How to Win Friends and Influence People

Lesson 1

Gain insight into handling difficult people

Discover the keys to popularity

How young people can look for a job

&

What employers want in their employees.

This book is a transcription of the original

Dale Carnegie's Radio Program

© Copyright 2006 – BN Publishing

www.bnpublishing.com

info@bnpublishing.com

Transcription: Deena W.

Printed in the U.S.A.

Gain insight into handling
difficult people

"Tune in" to Dale Carnegie's live radio broadcast in a particularly amusing edition of "How to Win Friends and Influence People". Gain insight into handling difficult people through the personal exploits of Dale Carnegie's guests, and benefit from learning Carnegie's "How to Win Rule" of the week on the futility of letting ourselves get upset by trivialities.

ANNOUNCER

COLGATE SHAVE CREAMS
PRESENT DALE CARNEGIE, the man
who can answer your problem! Millions
of readers profit by reading Dale
Carnegie's daily column of helpful advice
in more than one hundred of America's
leading newspapers; and his famous
book, "HOW TO WIN FRIENDS AND
INFLUENCE PEOPLE" has sold more
copies during its first eighteen months of
publication than any other non-fiction
book in all history. Now Colgate brings
Dale Carnegie's inspiring advice to you,
on the radio, so everyone can take
advantage of his proven rules for winning
happiness and success.

Now, Colgate Shave Creams present Dale Carnegie, <u>in person</u>!

CARNEGIE

Good evening, everyone!

If you think you have difficulties in winning friends and influencing people, just listen to the story of Cliff Sabrey. Cliff Sabrey is cruise director for the Cunard White Star Line. Each year he takes three or four hundred people on a world tour, visiting every continent washed by the seven seas. And the most important part of his job is to keep these people happy and contented under all sorts of conditions.

Cliff Sabrey is here in the studio, and in about 14 seconds he is going to step up in front of this microphone and tell you some of the things he has learned about handling difficult and unreasonable people. Mr. Sabrey, you must get some mighty strange demands from people when you're half way around the world, and a thousand miles from nowhere.

SABREY

Yes, most people are good sports, Mr. Carnegie, but others...! Well, you'd be amazed to see how some people react when they get off the beaten track. It's easy enough to be pleasant when you have all the conveniences we're used to in America – electric lights, shower baths, ice water. But naturally you can't get all these things at the far ends of the earth –

and that's when human nature begins to tell.

CARNEGIE
Yes, I'll bet it is.

SABREY
Take, for example, one woman who was with us on a world cruise, Mr. Carnegie. You know the type – nothing seemed to please her. I was taking one hundred and thirty people by train to see the Victoria Falls on the Zambesi River in South Africa – one of the most breathtaking sights on earth. The other one hundred and twenty-nine people were perfectly happy and contented. But not this woman. The train was only 15 minutes out of Johannesburg when she sent for me…

CARNEGIE

Ladies and gentlemen, what happened when Mr. Sabrey answered this woman's call is so interesting and so amusing – yet at the same time so instructive – that I have asked our actors here to dramatize the scene. For obvious reasons, we can't use the woman's real name, so we'll call her Mrs. Smith. All right, let's imagine we are on that train in Africa bound for Victoria Falls. Mrs. Smith has sent for Mr. Sabrey. Let's hear what she has to say:

(EFFECT: TRAIN CHUGGING)

MRS. SMITH

Mr. Sabrey, if you think for one minute that I'm going to put up with this for eight days and eight nights you've got another think coming!

SABREY

Why, what's wrong Mrs. Smith?

MRS SMITH

Huh! What's wrong! Just listen to the
noise from that engine! I spend more than
four thousand dollars to come on this trip
and you put me in a car right behind the
engine!

SABREY

But Mrs. Smith, you made your
reservation at the last minute, so
naturally, you got the last compartment
available.

MRS. SMITH

Well, I'm not going to stand for this!
You've got to do something! I shall write
your home office and report this outrage!

I shall be a nervous wreck! I –

SABREY

But Mrs. Smith, what would <u>you</u> do in my place?

MRS. SMITH

Why, I don't know! But do something – <u>anything</u>! Why can't you put the engine on the back of the train?

SABREY

But the…did you say, put the <u>engine</u> on the <u>back</u> of the train?

MRS. SMITH

Why, certainly! I've seen it done lots of times in America! You simply <u>push</u> the train instead of <u>pulling</u> it!

SABREY

But Mrs. Smith, we don't own the railroad, you know – we simply charter the train for this side-trip.

MRS. SMITH

Then wire the railroad! Get permission! Do something! I can't stand that noise, I tell you, and I won't! Why, I've traveled all over the United States and Europe, and I've never received such treatment before! Do you know who I am?

SABREY

Well, now, Mrs. Smith. I do realize who you are, and for that reason I am especially sorry that you should suffer this inconvenience. But after all, we are in Africa. And I am certain that a person who has traveled as extensively as you have, will realize that sometimes we can't avoid these little annoyances.

MRS. SMITH

Little annoyances! You call….

SABREY

Mrs. Smith, a person of your experience will be able, I'm sure, to understand my position. I admit you have a cause for complaint. But – may I offer you a sporting proposition?

MRS. SMITH

Well –

SABREY

If you'll put up with this racket – and frankly, I admit it is a racket – for the next few days, I'll go out of my way to make it up to you for the rest of the entire trip. When we get to the next hotel, I'll see that you have the finest room available – an outside room with a splendid view.

MRS. SMITH

A view is all very fine, Mr. Sabrey. But if you don't mind, I should prefer a private bath. At the last hotel…

SABREY

Fortunately, Mrs. Smith, at the <u>next</u> hotel I can provide you with <u>both</u> a view and a bath. Now, if you'll cooperate with me during this train-trip, I'll promise you that the rest of your trip will be one long delightful holiday. Now, is it a deal?

MRS.   SMITH   (MELTING RELUCTANTLY)

Well… I suppose I haven't much choice, Mr. Sabrey. But I would appreciate it if you'd give me extra attention in the future. I simply can't enjoy myself if I'm not comfortable.

SABREY

Thank you, Mrs. Smith. I knew I could rely on your sportsmanship. And wait until you see Victoria Falls – (FADING) They're twice as high as Niagara and twice as beautiful, and…
(EFFECT: ENGINE SOUNDING OUT)

CARNEGIE

Well, congratulations, Mr. Sabrey, on the way you handled a very difficult situation. But when Mrs. Smith told you to move the engine, I'll bet you felt like asking her who in the blazes she thought she was!

SABREY

Yes, I surely did. For a minute I could hardly believe my ears. But if I had told her how utterly impossible she was being, she'd have left the party at the next stop. As it was, we got along beautifully the rest of the cruise, and when Mrs. Smith went around the world again, she booked her passage with my company.

CARNEGIE

So by holding your temper for a few minutes you really earned your company another four thousand dollars from the same customer!

SABREY

Yes, that's right. You know, Mr. Carnegie, I've been taking people all over the face of the earth for the last nine years, but I never get over being surprised at one thing.

CARNEGIE

What's that?

SABREY

Simply that people will save their money for years and travel thousands of miles just to see some wonderful sight – like Mount Everest, for example, or the temple ruins at Angkor – and then will spoil their enjoyment of these sights by fussing and fretting over the little things – trivialities – that no one can help.

CARNEGIE (LAUGHING)

Well, you don't have to go around the world to encounter that attitude. In every walk of life you will find that two people can meet the same situation, and one will rise above it and have a good time out of it, and the other will make himself sick over it, by complaining and feeling sorry for himself. Let me give you an example, from my own experience. I took a cruise to Nova Scotia last summer, and the last night out was a gala occasion. The stewards passed out tin horns and noisemakers. The passengers wore paper hats and wandered from table to table singing. Sure, it was noisy, but the majority of the passengers were having a good time. But one man there was having a miserable time. He complained to the waiter. He wanted the noise stopped. He fidgeted and fumed until everyone around him wished he would go and jump into the Atlantic Ocean. Finally, in disgust, he left the table and went to his own stateroom without finishing his dinner.

Now, I happened to know that man was extremely wealthy, and he had traveled all over the world. But with all his wealth and travel he hadn't learned one of the first lessons in life – that we must adjust ourselves to our surroundings. We must not expect everyone else to act according to <u>our</u> desires.

SABREY

I've seen that same incident a hundred times, Mr. Carnegie, all over the world. And I have always felt sorry for these people, because they <u>could</u> enjoy themselves, if they'd change their mental attitude.

CARNEGIE

Right, Mr. Sabrey! And to show what mental attitudes can do, here's a story told me by a friend of mine, Vash Young. A short time ago, Vash Young made a trip to Knoxville, Tenn. Everything on that trip went wrong. First of all, he was kept awake all night in the train by a baby that was fussing and crying. Naturally, he was annoyed. But he said to himself:

"Listen, I can't sleep. But think of that mother. Maybe the child is ill, and the mother is worried. Isn't <u>her </u>situation worse than mine?" So he refused to let a sleepless night upset him. When he reached Knoxville, he found that a football game was being held there that day and he couldn't get a taxi. He could have got into a fine flurry over this, but he didn't. He said to himself: "Well, at least the cab drivers are doing a good business. And anyhow, a walk won't hurt me." So he carried his bags to the hotel himself. When he got to the hotel, he had to wait in line for a room, and <u>then</u> he was shown to a room that was still in disorder. The bed hadn't even been made!

Vash Young told me later: "By this time I <u>really</u> had to control myself. I was tempted to raise the roof. Instead, I stood in the middle of the room and said to myself: See here, Vash Young, are you going to let that unmade bed force you to make a fool of yourself? Are you going to let a pile of rumpled blankets triumph over you and make you lose your temper and your peace of mind?"

No, of course not. So he quietly telephoned, and asked them to send up a maid as soon as possible.

Vash Young is a philosopher – the kind of philosopher every man ought to be. He realized that all the stewing and fretting in the world wouldn't bring him what he wanted, but possibly what he did not want – a headache and exasperation.

Ladies and gentlemen, now, just what have we got from listening to Mr.

Sabrey's experiences that you and I can use tomorrow? First, we have gained some extremely helpful advice on how to handle a person when we really have to say "No". And we have learned the futility of letting ourselves be upset by trivialities.

What if your stenographer does do a letter wrong and you have to dictate it over again? What if the groceries <u>do</u> arrive late from the store? What if you <u>do</u> miss your streetcar or bus, and have to wait for the next one? Is flying into a rage going to change any of these things? No, it won't change anything on earth but your nerves and your own peace of mind.

So let's make this our How to Win Rule for this week: "Remember that trivialities are, after all – only trivialities. And you owe it to yourself to rise above such petty annoyances, and refuse to let them make you unhappy and distressed."

Now, if you have some problems which we may be able to help you solve, or if you have benefited from any of the principles we have been discussing on this program, won't you please write to me, Dale Carnegie, care of the National Broadcasting Company, New York City. If your story is one that will be of help or interest to our listeners, I shall invite you to appear before this microphone and share your story with our coast-to-coast audience just as Mr. Sabrey has done tonight.

ANNOUNCER

Dale Carnegie will be back in a moment to tell you about next Saturday's broadcast.

Now, people all over America have spent <u>thousands of dollars</u> for Dale Carnegie's secret of how to win friends! But, on this program, Colgate actually <u>gives</u> you his inspiring advice. And all we ask is one thing. Won't you simply <u>try</u> Colgate Brushless or Colgate Rapid Shave Cream – the amazing products that make this program possible? Then <u>you </u>will get the cool, easy shave that thousands of men now enjoy!

Now, Dale, what <u>are</u> you going to talk about next Saturday?

CARNEGIE (TEASER HERE)

You may not be a boss, nor a secretary, but the principles we are going to discuss here the next week will help you realize why people like or dislike you, regardless of whether you are a banker or a barber or a mother or a chauffeur.

Good night, everyone.

ANNOUNCER
Tune in again next Saturday evening, at this same hour, when Colgate Shave Creams will again present Dale Carnegie in "How To Win Friends and Influence People". Ben Grauer speaking. This is the National Broadcasting Company.

Discover the keys to
popularity

Discover the keys to popularity and find out what makes people like or dislike you, in this insightful edition of Dale Carnegie's live radio show, "How to Win Friends and Influence People". Follow live interviews with five secretaries who share what they dislike about their bosses, and benefit from Dale Carnegie's five rules that will help you gain favor not only with your secretary, but with your wife, your children, your sweetheart, and everyone else.

ANNOUNCER

COLGATE SHAVE CREAMS PRESENT DALE CARNEGIE, the man who can answer your problem! Millions of readers profit by reading Dale Carnegie's daily column of helpful advice in more than one hundred of America's leading newspapers; and his book, "How to Win Friends and Influence People" has sold more copies during its eighteen months of publication than has any other non-fiction book in all history.

Now, Colgate brings you Dale Carnegie –
on the radio – so everyone in America can
learn his seven rules for winning
happiness and success! Also – to tell you
MEN how to get the most out of your
razor when you use a brushless shaving
cream!

Now, Colgate Shave Creams present Dale
Carnegie, in person!

CARNEGIE

Good evening, everyone ------

You know very few of us see ourselves as others see us. So the best way to find out what people think of us, is to ask the other fellow. For example, ask the average secretary what she things of her boss. Her estimate isn't just limited to the office – the boss acts the same wherever he is – at home, at the club, or out among his customers. So what a secretary thinks of the man she works for is what other people think of him too.

You may not be a boss, nor a secretary, but the principles we are going to discuss here tonight will help you realize why people like or dislike you, regardless of whether you are a banker or a barber or a mother or a chauffeur.

Well, what <u>do</u> secretaries think of the men they work for? Not long ago, the Katherine Gibbs School, one of the largest secretarial schools in America, with branches in New York, Boston and Providence, sent out a confidential questionnaire to more than one thousand secretaries from coast to coast. The answers to this questionnaire were perfectly frank, for the school promised that neither the names of the secretaries nor of the firms for which they worked would ever be made public. I wasn't shown the questionnaires, but I was given ten pages of typewritten material summarizing what these girls liked and didn't like about their employers. I was so intrigued by this information that I went out and interviewed a number of secretaries myself this week. I have five of these girls here in the studio now; and they are going to step in front of this microphone and tell you what they dislike about the men they work for.

I'm not going to introduce these girls by name. I'm merely going to call them by number.

All right, here is Secretary Number One: won't you please tell us about your boss? What do you dislike about him?

ONE

I dislike my boss because he is a sourpuss. He usually comes down to the office with a grouch on. He never smiles. He never asks me how I am feeling. Sometimes he doesn't even say "good morning". He hurts my feelings by barking orders at me when other people are around. He doesn't hand me work to do. He throws it at me.

CARNEGIE

You can be thankful for one thing. You can be thankful you are his secretary and not his wife. Can you imagine what that man does to his family when he gets home? There is an old Chinese proverb that says, "A man who doesn't smile shouldn't keep a shop." And he shouldn't be a boss either. Old-fashioned cheerfulness is a priceless asset both in business and social life. For example, I sometimes have breakfast at a large restaurant on 42cd Street. There are over a dozen waitresses in that restaurant, but two of them stand out above all the others. Why? Because they are always smiling. They radiate welcome and good nature. They make my breakfast a ceremony of morning cheerfulness. Is it any wonder that I always make it a point to sit at the table served by one of those two girls? They give me no better service than anyone else, and they bring me the same food. But they do it with such good spirit that the same food actually tastes better.

I want to get up a set of rules tonight on how to avoid getting yourself generally disliked. So here is rule number one: IF you want to be popular, don't be a sourpuss.

All right, Secretary Number Two, will you step up to the microphone please. What do you dislike about your boss?

TWO

Well, I dislike the fact that I never get home on time. He makes me work overtime almost every night. I wouldn't mind if it were really necessary, but it isn't. He hates to dictate letters so he puts off dictating his mail until after four o'clock. Then I have to stay till 6:30 to 7:00 at night to get the letters typed. I know he means well, but he is just thoughtless.

CARNEGIE

Yes, there are lots of people like that. They never think about what other people want. They think only of what they want. And these people are never popular. For example, I was having dinner with some friends not long ago. There were eight people present. One man wanted to go down in the basement and play ping-pong. Nobody else had the slightest interest in playing ping-pong. But did that faze him? No sir, he just kept on insisting until finally all of us had to go down to the basement and watch him play ping-pong; and we all secretly hoped we would never be invited to a dinner party again where he was present. So, if you want to be popular, rule two is: Consider other people's desires and wishes. Don't insist on doing only what <u>you</u> want to do.

All right, here is Secretary Number Three. What do you dislike about your boss?

THREE
Well, I like my present boss, Mr. Carnegie, but let me tell you about a former boss of mine. I used to work for a large publishing house. I worked every

Sunday and took Mondays off. I dropped in to my office one Monday to get something on my desk; and the publisher asked me if I would write four or five letters for him. That wasn't my job, but naturally I said, "Yes, I'd be glad to do it."

He didn't dictate the letters – he simply gave me the gist of what he wanted to say. There were personal letters, letters to friends of his, and required a good deal of thought and tact in composing them. When I took the letters to his desk, do you think he bothered to thank me for taking time from my day off to do him a favor? No. He merely read the letters through, signed them, then threw them back at me and said, "Mail them." That man's a big shot in the publishing world, Mr. Carnegie, but I'd hate to tell you just how small he is in my estimation. What's more, that happened seven or eight years ago, and I'm <u>still</u> sore about it.

CARNEGIE

So you are burned up about it eight years later, are you? Well, I know precisely how you feel.

Now contrast that man with Owen D. Young, Chairman of the Board of the General Electric Company. Owen D. Young was getting off a Pullman sleeper in Florida. He had had an enjoyable and restful trip from New York, and the Pullman porter had been courteous and attentive. Owen D. Young gave him a generous tip and then said: "I wish I could always be sure of doing my job as perfectly as you do yours."

Did Owen D. Young mean what he said? Of course he meant it. No man handling the complex and confounding problems that Owen D. Young wrestles with, could even hope to come as near to perfection as that porter did.

Mr. Young's words of appreciation did four things. First, they made the porter happy. Second, because they made the porter happy, they also gave Owen D. Young a feeling of satisfaction. Third, they inspired the porter to want to continue to do a splendid job. And fourth, they impressed me so much that I am telling them to you; and as result of that, I hope that people living down in Texas and Tennessee and out in California, will be moved to give a few extra words of appreciation tomorrow.

So if you want to be popular, rule three is: Don't forget to say: "Thank You". Don't treat your employees as if they were so many slaves.

All right, here's Secretary Number Four. Won't you please tell us what you dislike about your boss?

GIRL NO. FOUR
Well, Mr. Carnegie, my boss is always complaining, always telling everybody how hard he works, and how tired he is, and how nobody appreciates all he does. He goes around saying, "I'm the neck of the bottle. Everything has to come out of me. Why can't somebody else do something right for a change? Why do I have to be driven crazy?"

CARNEGIE (LAUGHING)

Well, that man is affected with the devastating disease of self-pity. He ought to remember there are only four persons on earth who are interested in hearing about your troubles. Who are they? Why, they are your mother, your preacher, your doctor, and your lawyer. And remember, your doctor and your lawyer are <u>paid</u> for listening to your troubles.

I telephoned yesterday to the Reverend Oliver M. Butterfield, here in New York City. He is one of the foremost authorities on marriage in America, and he has devoted years to studying the causes of marriage disasters. I asked Dr. Butterfield if this matter of self-pity, and martyr complex, and blaming everybody but yourself – I asked him how much they had to do with divorce. He said that self-pity was a tremendously important factor in divorce.

So, if you want to be popular, rule four is: "Don't go around pitying yourself and whining about your troubles."

All right. Here's Secretary Number Five. What do you dislike about your boss?

FIVE
Well, I have a terrible boss, Mr. Carnegie. He is so conceited. Nobody likes him. He is always talking about how big he is.

CARNEGIE
Yes, I know the type. Thinks he can play better golf than anybody else. Can catch more fish and tell funnier stories than anyone else!

GIRL

Yes, and he's the world's best writer of advertising copy. Why, I actually heard him say once in a public talk that he had always been successful in everything he had ever undertaken; and he is always belittling other people and bragging about the great things he is going to do.

CARNEGIE

Well, a famous philosopher said 200 years ago that when a man falls in love with himself, it is generally the beginning of a lifelong romance.

You know, your boss reminds me of General John Pope. During the Civil War, Lincoln put General Pope in charge of the army on the Potomac. Pope immediately issued a proclamation to the army bragging about all the victories he had won in the West. And he insinuated that the soldiers there on the Potomac were a lot of infernal cowards. Mind you, he actually condemned the soldiers who were expected to fight for him, and then boasted about all the military miracles he was going to perform.

He issued so many bombastic announcements he was soon called "Proclamation Pope". What happened? His officers and men despised him. He was about as popular as a diamond-backed rattlesnake.

Now that happened seventy-five years ago. But I'll bet there is hardly a business house in America that hasn't at some time or another had its little "Proclamation Pope", bragging about the miracles he was going to perform.

So here is rule five: "If you want people to like you, don't go around bragging about how smart <u>you</u> are, and telling other people about your brilliant achievements".

Now you five girls have told us what a boss should do to get along with his secretary. Now here's something you can do to make a friend of your boss. Won't each of you give your boss one of these tubes of Colgate Shave Cream?

GIRLS
Thank you, Mr. Carnegie. (etc.)

CARNEGIE
I hope I haven't given the impression tonight that all secretaries dislike their bosses, for I was very much impressed by the number of secretaries who talked at

length about what they liked in the men they worked for, and I hope to give a broadcast about that subject some other time.

And now, let's summarize the five points brought out by the five secretaries we have just listened to. If you want to be popular, not only with your secretary, but with your wife, your child, your sweetheart, and everyone else, here's the way to do it:

Rule 1: Don't be a sourpuss. Smile. Radiate cheerfulness, and people will be glad to see you come in, and sorry to see you leave.

Rule 2: Consider other people's desires and wishes. Don't insist on doing only what you want to do.

Rule 3: Never take favors for granted. Always say "thank you" and people will go out of their way to serve you.

Rule 4: Don't go around pitying yourself and whining about your troubles. Remember other people have tribulations too.

Rule 5: Don't go around telling people how smart you are and bragging about your brilliant achievements. Let other people find out for themselves what a great guy you are.

GRAUER
Dale it seems to me you're being pretty hard on the bosses tonight.

CARNEGIE

Well, Ben, just to make up for that, I'm going to give another broadcast soon on the <u>other</u> side of the question. Then we'll find out what bosses don't like about their employees.

And let me add that if any of our listeners have been benefiting from the rules we discuss here every Saturday night, or if <u>you</u> have some problem we may be able to help you solve, won't you please write to me, Dale Carnegie, care of the National Broadcasting Company, New York City. If your story is one that will be of help to our other listeners, we shall invite you to appear before this microphone and share your story with our coast-to-coast audience.

ANNOUNCER

Dale Carnegie will be back in a moment to tell you about <u>next</u> Saturday's broadcast.

But first, please remember that Dale Carnegie is on the radio just <u>to help you</u>! And – the way to show your appreciation for Dale's advice on winning new friends and new success – is to try his products – <u>Colgate BRUSHLESS Shave Cream</u> or <u>Colgate RAPID Shave Cream!</u>

-

I know you'll be glad you did! For example – if you use a <u>lather</u> cream – a <u>single</u> trial with Colgate Rapid Shave Cream will prove that here is truly a "friendly" shave…an easy, <u>painless</u> shave that makes your face <u>feel</u> like smiling and wining friends!

Here is the <u>reason</u> that Colgate Rapid Shave Cream brings you this new shaving comfort! It makes a more <u>scientific</u> lather that <u>soaks</u> whiskers soft, right down to the skin-line!

With whiskers soft, you can shave as <u>close</u> as you want – yet there's no pull, no scrape from your razor! Your face is left <u>cool</u> and <u>smooth</u> as velvet! That's why Colgate Rapid Shave Cream is replacing "<u>old-fashioned</u>" lather creams so fast!

So get Colgate <u>Rapid </u>Shave Cream or Colgate <u>Brushless</u> Cream from any drug counter with this amazing guarantee! If you do not agree that Colgate brings you sensational new shaving comfort – you can get <u>double</u> your money back by sending empty tube to Colgate at Jersey City, New Jersey!

Now, Dale, what _are_ you going to talk about next Saturday?

CARNEGIE

You know, Ben, there are twenty-one million young people in the country between the ages of sixteen and twenty-four, who are wondering what they are going to do with their future. That means that there is hardly a home in America that isn't facing the problem of what to do about these youngsters – and it's a problem that not only concerns the youngsters themselves and their parents, but employers, voters and taxpayers the country over. That includes all of us, Ben. So next week we are going to present Dr. Homer P. Rainey, head of the American Youth Commission, who is going to help us find a solution to this problem.

ANNOUNCER

Tune in next Saturday at this same hour –
when Colgate Shave Creams will again
present Dale Carnegie in "How to Win
Friends and Influence People!" Ben
Grauer speaking. This is the Red Network
of the National Broadcasting Company.

CARNEGIE

Let's summarize the five points brought out by the five secretaries we have just listened to. If you want to be thoroughly unpopular, not only with your secretary, but with your wife, your child, your sweetheart, and everybody else, here's a way to do it.

Rule 1: Be a sourpuss. Never smile. Be as cheerful as a grizzly bear with rheumatism in his hind legs.

Rule 2: Don't consider other people's desires or their wishes. "Other people" aren't important. You are the big chief in your bailiwick. So insist on doing only what <u>you</u> want to do.

Rule 3: Take all favors for granted. Never say "thank you" to anyone. Treat your employees as if they were so many slaves, and be interested only in yourself.

Rule 4: Go around pitying yourself and whining about your troubles.

Rule 5: If you want to be absolutely positive of being unpopular, go around telling people how smart you are, and brag one hundred percent about your brilliant achievements.

How young people can look for a job

In yet another inspiring edition of Dale Carnegie's live radio broadcasts on "How to Win Friends and Influence People", Dale Carnegie tackles the problem of "the future" faced by twenty-one million American boys and girls between the ages of sixteen and twenty-four –and tries to find the solution. Don't miss Carnegie's tips on free youth services, and his advice on how young people can go about more intelligently looking for a job, and how they can get an education with little or no money.

ANNOUNCER

COLGATE SHAVE CREAM PRESENTS DALE CARNEGIE - the man who can answer your problem! Millions of readers profit by reading Dale Carnegie's daily column of helpful advice in more than one hundred of America's leading newspapers; and his book, "How to Win Friends and Influence People" has sold more copies during its eighteen months of publication than has any other non-fiction book in all history. Now Colgate brings you Dale Carnegie, <u>on</u> <u>the</u> <u>radio</u>, so his inspiring advice can also help <u>YOU</u> find new happiness and success!

Now Colgate Shave Creams present Dale Carnegie, in person!

CARNEGIE

Good evening, everyone…

Tonight we are going to discuss a problem that faces one-sixth of the population of the United States. And that problem is: How can American youth find its place in the world today? One person in every six in this county is between the age of sixteen and twenty-four. This means there is hardly a home from Portland, Oregon, to Portland, Maine that hasn't some young member of the family saying: "I've finished school. Now what? Where do I go from here?"

I know exactly how these boys and girls feel, because I was in the same position myself once. So the whole purpose of this program tonight is to tell these young people two things: first, how they can go about more intelligently looking for a job; and second, how they can get an education with little or no money.

If these youths of America will listen to this program they will be pleasantly surprised to discover how many free services they can get to help them forge ahead in life. So please get a pencil and paper now, for you will want to take down some addresses later.

The makers of Colgate Shave Cream have joined with me in bringing to the studio tonight, Dr. Homer P. Rainey, director of the American Youth Commission. For the past three years, Dr. Rainey and his assistants have been making an exhaustive study of these twenty-one million boys and girls between sixteen and twenty-four – finding out what their problems are, and trying to find the solution.

Dr. Rainey, suppose one of these twenty-one million youngsters came to you and asked you how to get a job? What would you tell him?

RAINEY
First of all, I would tell him to find out what he can do best; for that's the line he is most likely to succeed in.

CARNEGIE
But suppose a boy doesn't know what he is fitted for? How can he find out?

RAINEY

The government is setting up vocational guidance services under the WPA in practically every city in the country. If a boy doesn't know where his nearest vocational guidance service is, he can write to the American Youth Commission, Washington, D.C. and we shall be glad to tell him.

CARNEGIE

Well, Dr. Rainey, suppose a boy <u>does</u> go to his U.S. Employment Services, just exactly what do they do for him?

RAINEY

They give him all kinds of tests to find out what he can do best, Mr. Carnegie. They give him psychological tests, aptitude tests, and try to discover whether he is good at figures or mechanics or, say, writing advertising. One youngster was making a miserable flop of his job as a bookkeeper. He detested figures. The vocational guidance services discovered that, with his particular personality and aptitudes, he ought to be a salesman, and today he is making much more money than before, and is much happier.

CARNEGIE
And it doesn't cost a penny to get all this service?

RAINEY
No, it is paid for by the government, Mr. Carnegie.

CARNEGIE
Well, suppose a girl wants to be a nurse, for example, or a boy wants to be a civil engineer, and they don't have any

training. How can they find out what training they need, and what their chances are of earning a living in that field?

RAINEY

The United States office of Education at Washington, D.C. issues leaflets on nineteen different professions, Mr. Carnegie – from journalism to how to be a horse doctor. These leaflets tell you what you can expect in each profession, how much training you need, what the opportunities are, and what salary you can hope to make. And these leaflets cost only a nickel each.

CARNEGIE

Well, suppose a boy does know what he wants to do, and he does have the training – how does he go about finding a job?

RAINEY

The United States Employment Service has set up free employment agencies all over the country. Every city has one. And all cities have Junior Placement Services especially for young people without experience.

CARNEGIE

But suppose a boy or girl lives – say, in Maryville, Missouri – or some other country town far from a large city – how can they reach their nearest free employment agency? How can they find out where it is?

RAINEY

Again, Mr. Carnegie, if they write to us at the American Youth Commission, in Washington, we will be glad to tell them where their nearest United States

Employment Agency is located. And here's another thing few people realize – in some states, there are traveling employment services.

CARNEGIE
You mean traveling employment agencies that actually come to your own door, like traveling libraries?

RAINEY
Yes. So far, not every state has them. But one thing is certain – we <u>can</u> put every young person in contact with his nearest free employment agency.

CARNEGIE
How many of our young people are looking for work, Dr. Rainey?

RAINEY

Around five million, and only a little more than half of them are finding jobs.

CARNEGIE

Won't you tell us - why will some applicants be given preference over others?

RAINEY

First, because of skill and ability. The man who knows his job, who is mater of his trade or profession, will naturally get first preference when people are being hired. Second, determination. The man who keeps up his enthusiasm, his confidence, his determination to succeed, certainly has an edge on the chap who is licked by discouragement. But another very big factor of all in getting jobs is personality.

CARNEGIE

And personality, after all, is just one thing: the impression you make on people. A recent survey showed that three-fourths of all the young people who get fired, are fired simply because they can't get along with other people.

Now Dr. Rainey, suppose a young person said to you: "I've just got out of high school. I haven't any money, and I haven't any job. What shall I do – find a job, or try to go to college?" What would you tell him?

RAINEY

I'd tell him to go to college, by all means, if possible, and if he has good reason to believe that college will be beneficial to him.

CARNEGIE

And work his way through?

RAINEY

Certainly, Mr. Carnegie. One-fifth of all the students in our colleges today are working their way through with little or no money.

CARNEGIE

Well, I've got here in the studio, Dr. Rainey, a young man who wants to meet you. I asked him here because I think he is representative of those young people who can't be licked by anything. He's only seventeen years old, yet he has actually worked his way through high school. His name is Harold Socks and hi lives in Brooklyn, New York.

Will you step up to the microphone, Mr. Socks?

HAROLD

Good evening, Mr. Carnegie.

CARNEGIE

Harold, will you tell Dr. Rainey your story, just as you told it to me?

HAROLD

Well, Dr. Rainey, my father died two years ago, and left my mother and two sisters and myself without any money. After father died, I quit school and worked as a helper to an upholsterer. But my salary was so small that I realized I was foolish not to get an education. So I went back to high school. Our high school has eleven counselors who spend all their time helping students. They help

73

us decide what we want to study, and if we need part-time jobs, they help us find them. So I told my counselor what my situation was; they helped me find outside work, and I supported myself through school by doing all kinds of odd jobs.

CARNEGIE
Tell Dr. Rainey some of the things you did, Harold.

HAROLD
Oh, I was an errand boy, a soda clerk, I worked in a grocery store, and I waited on tables in the school lunch room.

RAINEY
And now you have your diploma?

HAROLD
Yes, sir. I graduated this last week, and

this fall I'm going to college. I'm going to study forestry.

RAINEY

Forestry! That's a strange subject for a city boy to take up.

HAROLD

I suppose it is, Dr. Rainey. But I used to spend the summers on my Uncle's farm, and I have learned to love trees.

RAINEY

Well, forestry is a promising field for a young man these days. Flood control and the prevention of droughts is going to require young men with an expert knowledge of forestry. What college are you going to?

HAROLD

Syracuse University – they have a good forestry course there and it's a state college, so I won't have to pay any tuition.

RAINEY

Do you know that the National Youth Administration has set up a huge fund to be used by colleges in giving part-time employment to students in your situation? Each college is authorized to give employment to twelve percent of their students, and the salary is fifteen dollars a month.

HAROLD

I've made applications for that, Dr. Rainey, and I intend to find other work besides to pay for my extra expenses.

RAINEY

Don't worry – you'll get through. When I started for college, I had so little money I had to borrow my train fare from my grandmother's pension! I earned my room and board by working for a man who ran a seed store. And I remember I did everything from packaging seeds and milking cows to tending the baby! I've compared notes with dozens of other men who worked their way through college, and well all agree we were better off for having to work.

CARNEGIE

There are thousands of boys and girls listening to this broadcast who long to go to college and who have no money whatever. How can they do it? Well, I was in that same position thirty years ago and I can tell you how I did it.

I attended a State Teacher's College at Warrensburg, Missouri where I didn't have to pay any tuition. Is there such a college in your state? Yes, there's <u>at</u> <u>least</u> one in every state.

But suppose you do go to a state-supported college where there are no fees? How can you earn your board and room? Personally, I lived on a farm and rode a plough-horse three miles to college every day, and then galloped back home at night and milked the cows and chopped the firewood and studied my lessons by the light of a coal oil lamp.

Go to almost any college town and tell the college authorities that you want to work for your board and room. They may send you to someone who wants your services. If not, then visit every merchant and prosperous-looking house in town. You will find someone who will gladly give you board and room in return for a few hours work per day. Or go and call on the surrounding farmers and offer to milk the cows and do the chores in return for your board and room.

Many of the most famous and successful men in America today have worked their way through college. Take Lowell Thomas, for example. Her worked his way through four universities by tending furnaces, acting as a cook and waiter, feeding cows, selling real estate, and doing a bit of teaching on the side.

Rest assured of one thing. You can and will work your way through college if you only want to badly enough.

Dr. Rainey, may I say on behalf of my sponsors, the makers of Colgate Shave Cream, I consider it a great privilege to have you here tonight to give this information to the millions of our listeners whom you know and I know are in vital need of it.

This program is made possible, by the way, by Colgate Shave Cream. Here is a tube of it. I think you will like it.

RAINEY
Thank you, Mr. Carnegie.

CARNEGIE
Now let's see if we can't summarize quickly the points we have make tonight.

First: If a boy doesn't know what vocation he wants to follow, he should go to his nearest branch of the U.S. Employment Service for advice. And if he doesn't know where that is, he can write to the American Youth Commission, Washington, D.C.

Secondly: If he does know what he wants to do, but needs more information about his chosen vocation, he can write to the Office of Education at Washington and secure a leaflet on that subject for five cents.

Third: If he wants to go to college, and has no money, he can <u>earn</u> his way by going to one of the free state colleges that charge no tuition, and he can apply to the National Youth Administration for a part-time job to help pay his outside expenses.

CLOSING

ANNOUNCER

Dale Carnegie will be back in a moment to tell you abut <u>next </u>Saturday's broadcast.

Now remember – Dale is on the air to help <u>you</u> win new friends – AND to win new friends for <u>Colgate</u> <u>Shave</u> <u>Cream</u>!

Now, Dale, what <u>are</u> you going to talk about next Saturday?

-

CARNEGIE

Next week we are going to have as one of our guests on this program, Mr. Ellis A. Gimbel, Jr., head of Gimbel's, one of New York's largest department stores. Mr. Gimbel is going to tell us how he wins friends and influences people, and he is going to tell you the qualities American business is looking for in employees.

ANNOUNCER

Tune in again next Saturday at this same hour, when Colgate Shave Creams will again present Dale Carnegie in "How To Win Friends and Influence People". Ben Grauer speaking. This is the Red Network of the National Broadcasting Company.

What employers want in their employees.

In this last broadcast of twenty-six weekly radio programs featuring Dale Carnegie and his "How To Win Rules", Dale Carnegie explores what employers want in their employees. Find out the three main points he brings out that you can use immediately to help you get a job, help you win recognition <u>in</u> your job, and help you deal with people more effectually in both in business and in your home.

And you won't to miss Dale Carnegie's GRAND SUMMARY of all of his rules on "How to Win Friends and Influence People" included in this special, final broadcast.

ANNOUNCER

COLGATE SHAVE CREAM PRESENTS DALE CARNEGIE, the man who can answer _your_ problem! Millions of readers profit be reading Dale Carnegie's daily copy of helpful advice in more than one hundred of America's leading newspapers; and his book, "How to Win Friends and Influence People" has sold more during its eighteen months of publication than has any other non-fiction book in all history.

Now, Colgate brings Dale Carnegie to you, on the radio!

Now, Colgate Shave Creams presents Dale Carnegie – in person!

CARNEGIE

Good evening, everyone…

Two weeks ago on this program we showed what qualities employees want in their employers. Tonight, we are going to show what employers want in their employees.

So I have invited to this studio tonight Mr. Ellis A. Gimbel, Jr., executive head of Gimbel's big New York department store, and vice-president of the Gimbel chain of department stores that extends from coast to coast. Mr. Gimbel employs between three to four thousand people in his New York store alone. His business brings him in daily contact with thousands of people. I have watched him at work, and know he is a master of human relations, so, in a moment, Mr.

Gimbel is going to step up in front of this microphone, and help us bring out three points that you can use immediately to help you get a job, help you win recognition in your job, and help you deal with people more effectually in both in business and in your home.

Mr. Gimbel, first of all, won't you please tell us what you, an employer of nearly four thousand people, are looking for in the people you hire?

GIMBEL

Well, Mr. Carnegie, most of our employees are sales people. We don't demand brilliance in our sales girls and we are not insistent on a college education, but do want people who can put their heart into their work and make the customers feel that it is a pleasure to serve them.

CARNEGIE

And how badly such salespeople are needed, Mr. Gimbel! Let me tell you what happened to me last week! I was walking down Fifth Avenue when a necktie in a store window caught my eye. I went into the store to buy it.

Several salespeople were idle, but no one greeted me at the door. I walked half way down the store until I reached a couple of salesmen lolling on the furniture, talking to one another. I had to stand in front of them before they even looked at me. Then one of them asked in a lifeless manner what I wanted. I told him I wanted a solid blue tie like the one displayed in the window. Did he offer to get it for me!? No. He looked toward the back of the store and yelled, "George – oh, George!"

George was evidently engaged, so with an air of resignation this chap condescended to wait on me himself. He pointed to a case of neckties and said: "See one in there you want?" I found one, and he walked away with it in a bored, listless manner and took so long to get it wrapped that I had to tell him I was in a hurry. Finally he handed me the package with a dreamy-eyed expression, as if he was thinking of the date he had that night, and he let me walk out of the store without even thanking me for my patronage. And mind you, that happened in a store on Fifth Avenue – one of the finest shopping streets on earth.

It seems incredible that in a big city like New York where hundreds of thousands of people are unemployed that it is difficult to get salespeople who will wait on customers in a way that will make the customer want to return to that store again.

GIMBLE

Yes, Mr. Carnegie, if people would only realize how much courtesy means to all of us, and how much faster they themselves would advance if they'd go out of their way to be courteous!

CARNEGIE

We mentioned on this program last week that there are twenty-one million young people in this country between the ages of 16 and 25. Many of them are unemployed and many of them are wondering how they can get a start in life. Well, one of the best ways I know of how to get a good flying start in business is be becoming a salesman. This is the way I started when I left college. Mr. Gimbel, do you think the field is overcrowded?

GIMBEL

It is overcrowded with incompetents, Mr. Carnegie. But it never has and it never will be overcrowded by the right kind of people.

CARNEGIE

Yes, business is always looking for salesmen who can go out and get orders – orders that will keep the smoke pouring out of factor chimneys. Good salesmen are in demand in good times, in hard times, and in all times. For example, Harold Sigmund, president of Afta Solvents Corporation, here in New York, told me that he advertises in the Sunday paper for salesmen and he has the big employment agencies send him men who want to sell. He even gives good men a drawing account against commission, and yet he finds it extremely difficult to get intelligent, neat-looking men with personality, who will go out and call on customers for eight hours a day, week in and week out, and use common sense and enthusiasm in selling his product. So here is the first point we want to bring out tonight. You men who are wondering how you can get started in business – let me suggest that you try salesmanship. Remember – it takes persistence. It takes personality. It takes self-confidence and hard work. But the rewards are great for those of you who are willing to play the game.

But this field isn't limited to young men only. I was talking last week with Mr. E. H. Little of Colgate's, head of the company that sponsors this program, and

Mr. Little told me that back in 1917 he had a group of young men selling Colgate's soap. Then suddenly the war came and his men were drafted into the army so he was forced to go out and hire salesmen who were 40 and 50 years old. And he said that those older men made one of the best sales forces he ever had.

GIMBEL

Well, Mr. Carnegie, we often find in many of our departments that a mature person has a definite advantage. For example, if a customer wants to buy something at the notion counter, she might prefer to waited on by a good looking girl. But if a customer is going to buy a fur coat, or some furniture, or a carpet she would much prefer to be waited on by a man or woman with experience and judgment. One of the biggest lessons I have learned is that too many young people will ruin a business – and too many old people will ruin it. Every business of any size should have both age and youth.

CARNEGIE

All right, then here's our second point. Youth and age must work together, for the advancement of both. Youth and age must collaborate. And don't think this applies only in business – it applies in the home, too, right inside your own family. Youth has energy, ideas and a driving ambition to get ahead – but youth can save itself a million headaches, and disappointments, if it will sit down and take counsel with age. And older men profit too if they let themselves be stimulated by the open-mindedness and undaunted enthusiasm of youth.

Now, Mr. Gimbel, you are looking for salespeople with enthusiasm and enterprise, and you also want the proper balance of age and youth in your organization. What else do you, as an employer, look for when you hire people?

GIMBEL

People with ideas, Mr. Carnegie. And you'll be pleased to know that some of our very best ideas come from people who are in relatively small positions. For example, we had a porter who tended the incinerator way down in the third basement. He came to us one day and said: "Look, I wonder if you realize how much stuff you throw away that could be used over again?" We said: "What do you mean?" And he said: "Oh, I know they don't look like much – old rusty fixtures and things like that. They're dumped downstairs because they're tarnished and all battered up, but isn't there some way they could be repaired? If you put a man down there to watch what goes on in that incinerator, you'll save an awful lot of money."

We said: "Fine! That's a good idea. You thought of it, so you're promoted. You take over the job."

CARNEGIE

So that porter, by thinking about his work, and keeping his eyes open, earned himself a raise in pay and a promotion, and saved the firm hundreds of dollars!

GIMBEL

That's right. Here's another example of an employee with ideas. We had a girl who was working as a copywriter in the advertising department. She came to us and complained that the shoulder straps on her slip kept falling over her shoulders when she had to hang on to a strap in a crowded subway;

She said if it happened to her it must happen to every woman. So with the help of a manufacturer we introduced a slip that overcame this difficulty. It was advertised from coast to coast, and women bought it by the thousands.

CARNEGIE

Ladies and gentlemen, here is the third point we want to bring out this evening. All employers are looking for people who are on the alert to discover new ways and means of improving the business. And it's these people – the people with ideas – who are the first to get a raise in pay, or a promotion. So why don't you look over your job tomorrow and see if there isn't some way you can save your employer money or time, or contribute to the efficiency of your organization?

Mr. Gimbel, I deeply appreciate – and I know our sponsor appreciates – your coming here tonight to help us give our listeners some practical pointers on how they can get ahead and improve themselves in their business careers. And here's something I wish you'd take along with you, Mr. Gimbel – a tube of Colgate Shave Cream.

GIMBEL

Thank you, Mr. Carnegie, I know it's good. I hope you sell a lot of it, and of course, if they buy it at Gimbel's, we won't mind.

CARNEGIE

Ladies and gentlemen, tonight concludes our last broadcast on this series of twenty-six programs for Colgate Shave Cream. For the past six months we have brought you each week some "How To Win Rule" which you could apply at once to help you get ahead, and to help you win friends and influence people.

On this last program, I have been asked to summarize some of these rules, so I have made up three sets of rules – four rules for winning friends, four rules for winning cooperation, and four rules for inspiring people to do their best work.

All right, here are the four rules for winning friends and making people like you.

Rule 1: Smile. Show people you are glad to see them; and they will be equally glad to see you.

Rule 2: Be vitally interested in remembering people's names for a man's name, to his own ears, is the sweetest sound in the world.

Rule 3: Be a good listener. Show a genuine, sincere interest in the other man and his affairs.

Rule 4: Be courteous! Let people realize that you deeply appreciate the little things they do for you, and don't just take them for granted.

And here are four rules for wining cooperation and getting people to see things your way.

Rule 1: Talk in terms of the other man's interest. Show him how, by doing things <u>your </u>way, he can get what he wants.

Rule 2: Don't criticize. Never tell a man he is wrong. If you do, you arouse his resentment, and cut off every avenue to his reason.

Rule 3: When you must correct errors, do it in such a way that the other man can always save his face.

Rule 4: Whenever possible, let the other man feel the idea you want to put across is partly <u>his</u> idea. You'll get further by using suggestion than you ever will be barking commandments.

And the third set of four rules are for getting the best out of a man, and inspiring him to do the best work he is capable of doing.

Rule 1: Be hearty in your approbation and lavish in your praise.

Rule 2: Show a man that you have a deep and sincere respect for his ability. Give him a feeling of importance.

Rule 3: Encourage him to do the thing he enjoys doing most, for that is the thing he will do best.

Rule 4: Give him a fine reputation to live up to, and show him that you confidently expect him to succeed.

Ladies and gentlemen:

These rules I have just read are not rules just to be heard over the air, and then forgotten. If they are followed out, they actually constitute a new way of life. But they must be studied – they must really be put into practice. And you and I and every one of us must check ourselves constantly to see that we are really making full use of them.

I cannot urge you too strongly to send and get your copy of these rules. You can then have a permanent record of them for yourself. You can study them at leisure during the summer months. You can make them a vital part of your daily life. And if you <u>do</u> do this, I can promise you that they will not only be of great help to you in solving your social problems, but they will pay you untold dividends in increased income, increased efficiency, and increased happiness.

It has been a real privilege and a real pleasure to be on this program each week for the last six months; and I do hope that some of the old truths that we have been discussing here have helped many of you lead richer and happier lives.

Good night, everyone – and lots of luck!

We have Book Recommendations for you

Dale Carnegie's Radio Program: How to
Win Friends and Influence People -Lesson 2

Dale Carnegie's Radio Program: How to
Win Friends and Influence People -Lesson 3

The Strangest Secret by Earl Nightingale
(Audio CD - Jan 2006)

Think and Grow Rich [MP3 AUDIO]
by Napoleon Hill, Jason McCoy (Narrator)

As a Man Thinketh [UNABRIDGED]
by James Allen, Jason McCoy (Narrator)

Thought Vibration or the Law of Attraction
in the Thought World [MP3 AUDIO]
by William Walker Atkinson, Jason McCoy

The Law of Success Volume I: The
Principles of Self-Mastery by Napoleon Hill

Thought Vibration or the Law of Attraction
in the Thought World & Your Invisible
Power (Paperback)

Automatic Wealth, The Secrets of the
Millionaire Mind-Including:As a Man
Thinketh, The Science of Getting Rich, The
Way to Wealth and Think and Grow Rich
(Paperback)

Get Published!

BN Publishing helped authors publish more titles. So whether you're writing a romance novel, historical fiction, mystery, action and suspense, poetry, children's or any other genre, we can help you reach your publishing goals.

Paperback

Reach 20,000 retail accounts in the U.S. (including chains, independents, specialty stories, and libraries).

Including:

www.amazon.com

www.amazon.co.uk

www.amazon.ca

www.bn.com

www.powells.com

www.ebay.com

and more...

Your book will be included in a physical catalog that will go out to over 20,000 retail stores.

When your title is entered into our library it will automatically appear in the bookstore and library databases.

Our United States and United Kingdom based sales teams works with publisher clients based throughout the world who want to print books in the United States and United Kingdom, or reach the North American, UK and wider European markets through our broad distribution channel partners.

If we decide to publish it:

we will send you 2 free copies of the finished book;

we will give you 10% royalty of the selling price of each book copy sold (selling price = the price the book is sold by BN Publishing to wholesalers or other resellers);

and if you wish to have more copies of your

book, we will sell you the book for two thirds of the list price.

Please send us more information about your book to info@bnpublishing.com